The Ishtar Gate

The Ishtar Gate

Sarah Corbett

First published 2025 by
Liverpool University Press
4 Cambridge Street
Liverpool
L69 7ZU

Copyright © 2025 Sarah Corbett

The right of Sarah Corbett to be identified as the author of this book has been asserted by her in accordance with the Copyright, Designs and Patents Act 1988.

All rights reserved. No part of this book may be reproduced, stored in a retrieval system, or transmitted, in any form or by any means, electronic, mechanical, photocopying, recording, or otherwise, without the prior written permission of the publisher.

British Library Cataloguing-in-Publication data
A British Library CIP record is available

The manufacturer's authorised representative in the EU for product safety is:
Easy Access System Europe, Mustamäe tee 50, 10621 Tallinn, Estonia
https://easproject.com (gpsr.requests@easproject.com)

ISBN 978-1-83624-457-8 softback

Typeset by lexisbooks.com
Printed and bound in Poland by Booksfactory.co.uk

A Triptych

because it is more interesting
                                        Krzysztof Kieślowski

And between these sounds, the silence speaks
        Anna Akhmatova, 'Poem Without a Hero'

For Gabrielle

Contents

The Ishtar Gate	1

I

Leningrad	4
Intervention (i), Mirror Work	5
Berlin	7
Leeds	8
Intervention (ii), Red	17
Ivo's House	10
Intervention (iii), Mirror	19
Sarajevo/Leeds	21

II

Intervention (iv), Cleaning the Bones	24
January	26
February	27
March	28
Intervention (v), Flag	29
April	31
May	32
June	33
Intervention (vi), Presence	34
July	35
August	36
September	37
Intervention (vii), Arrow	38
October	39

November			40
December			41
Intervention (viii), Seven Gates			42

III

1.	tonight the storm		46
2.	the day is cyan	de-oxygenated blue	46
3.	I write this	thirty years away	47
4.	everywhere	the voice of the air	47
5.	remember	when	48
6.	I walk out into the field		48
7.	a figure walks	shade of	49
8.	how will we know		49
9.	the other world	membrane	50
10.	debris of centuries	pile up	50
11.	daily I tread the meniscus	of water	51
12.	one day	I will join you	51
13.	what is Earth	but an ossuary	52
14.	what did I say		52
15.	I could sing	but my voice	53
16.	today at dawn	the crows return	53
17.	do you remember	the magpies	54
18.	I must speak	now of the trees	54
19.	I am become	water/	55
20.	listen	there is another	55

Notes	56
Acknowledgements	58

The Ishtar Gate

An Invocation to the Goddess –
Innana, Ishtar, Aphrodite, Venus

you wear lapis, jewel of the Earth
of dusk when Venus appears
      amidst the stars low
      in the west after sunset
queen of the heavens, lion-rider
owl-winged goddess, straddle here
      as we enter under
      dust-browned, war-trodden
love worn. We have crossed deserts
plains, hauled our cracked selves
      to this gate now a world-
      strewn monument, these
dragons, lions, flowers of the sun
one-horned bulls, all stolen fragments
resurrected in far museums
      to go under with you
      naked as newborns
in our skull-plates not the drum
of the mother but death's whisper
      see what you have not seen
      know what you do not know
dirt clots our toes, slates our hands
gluts our tongues, damps our eyes
      as behind us the horizons
      fracture and dissolve
we traverse the seven gates, songs
of the dead loud in our ears, until

       divested of all we harbour
       all armour, the underworld
takes us. three days your sister
hangs you until you rot, three days
       we wait until words
       again words wake you
we abandon shards of our many-
petalled hearts to rise through earth
         red-ears of corn
         white rays of flowers
         blue waters of the spring

I

Leningrad

New Year's Eve, 1940

imagined city, white city of the mind
        in the midnight of the year
                Anna Akhmatova
        sits in the house on the Fontanka
            at her window a maple
                    heavy with snow
            she is waiting. what is she
    waiting for? below, the river slips by
            black slick of the Neva
                  dark form of a dream
            where snow descends
dissolves as smoke

                    who speaks but the wind
            at the window extinguishing
    the candles? the mirror darkens
the poem begins … a musical phrase
            a voice overheard – shades
                of poets, lovers, a figure
    on the wall, chorus of ghosts
she cups an egg she is saving
        cool oval of shell, holds the interior
            of albumen and yolk
                as if she is holding
        the potential of the world

Intervention (i)

Mirror Work

after Wim Wenders, 'Wings of Desire' (1986)

she wanders the burnt-out circus tent
angel in chicken feather wings
and gold leather slippers treading
the ring of sawdust

                    thirty years

out of time

              still nineteen
in nineteen eighty-nine I slip through
                a hall of mirrors
                as on Prague's
                Petrin Hill

                          caught
                          in fragments
                          a tilting

labyrinth, an endless

                          fracturing
                          of selves

seeing but unable to
        recognise
        the lost girl, her dress woven
                with small mirrors
                as the new history
                unfolds in the wings

a loop of cinematic frames
                          she cannot escape

swinging back and forth on her trapeze
mane the lion of hope

                                      a flag waving
                                      in her red heaven

an about-to-be detonated

                                      landmine
                                      dreaming of love

Berlin

November 2019

city of the dead
streets of memories, memorials

and in my hotel room
on the first night the ghost
of my friend's daughter
in her hands a bowl of flowers

an echo rebounding
across the continent of sleep

after her my dead father
grandfather, grandmother
with whom I have a rendezvous
it seems. grandmother, what
do you want?

you taught me to play cards
and dust ornaments
until I broke the china vase
wreathed with flowers
the fragments haunting me for years

Leeds

November 1989

on the black and white TV
in the student kitchen
the grainy jubilance of the wall's
un-builders

....

night against the window
throws back our faces
my friend's long hair
her glasses' repeated glints
how young we are

....

night after night
we watch the fall
of stone and mortar
and after, the dancing

at the bombed church
workmen erect wooden houses
among nestfuls of cables
fake trees, conical
and ever-green

dim gold baubles
glühwein in metal pots
at the side of the road
cinnamon and sugar
names on brass disks

in the new church the statue
of a gold Christ swings
against a cauldron of blue
starlight of candles
in thousands of glass panes

and so a new world opens
like a fist

....

a parentheses of hope
within which I cannot rest

....

as when I was five and woke
to the singing of birds
in a sunlit midnight
between

Christmas and New Year
room of adults
cigarette smoke
and a voice that spoke
of the world on fire

step from the windblown Strasse
into a cold womb, blown egg
gun-metal chill of carved heads
walls of names, catacomb of names
everywhere underfoot the dead

move through grey-white daylight
thick with shrouds, in the Tiergarten
a spiral memorial, mausoleums among
the still trees at Wiessensee. see
grandmother, I am attending to the dead

in November I think of my father
the glottal stop of his heart that day
he was heard speaking to the winged
one who is invisible, dropped down
from the high tower

by the student halls
behind the supermarket
where the carpark runs
underground

....

past the industrial-
sized bins
where the Ripper's last victim
was found

....

we walk home
in pairs
our vulnerability as women
become women
fibrillating a dark heaven

from the hotel window
the railway line is a child's toy
under a sun-bleached rainbow
a mural of a cartoon dog
trains pulsing through

back and forth on lines
of time, loops of time
time opens and closes
according to its strange
magic. on the U Bahn

stations tick by
on my unfamiliar tongue
darkness unravelling
between stops that light up
briefly and vanish

the year I fall apart
arms a doll-death
head dropping to the road
legs can-can dancers
the conductor

of the orchestra
waving his baton at the air
ears clapping on emptiness
making a mess
of the music

heart flopping from my chest
slipping along tarmac
as the red horse of time
comes tripping
down the hill

(red horse of time, white horse of poetry, blue horse of dreams)

at the wall a boat along the Spree
where four swam East to West
getting nowhere but the other
side of the river where wind
beats out laughter

I walk all the way out and back
strange heads, hallucinations
*from the threshold of the sky
warmed still by corpses,* mushroom
cloud become sunburst, rainbow

over wine I read Bachmann
hear the possibility of poetry
as history sits inside me
and the remit of angels
is *assemble, testify, record*

a queue around the block
from the old cinema
our commencement
in a new history

....

a parcel of time
in each of our arms

....

oh
to be nineteen
on the cusp of the decade

....

what wings a turn
of the corner
might bring

Intervention (ii)

Red

after Krzysztof Kieślowski, 'Three Colours: Red' (1994)

who gives her the telephone, the dog, the coins
she collects all couched in red, red, drenched in red?
who gives her the dance, the absent lover, the old man/

young man who carries her destiny like a message
waiting in a book, her story bookended? she sits
in a movement of light *stay, the light is beautiful*

he says. what can we say takes place here? a glass
shatters, a window is blown by the storm, personal
weather that moves us into ourselves and away

follow the threads, red in the labyrinth, follow
the road that weaves over the hill, cable of song
under the waves. this is her gift – her sadness

her beauty, the press of her lips. each red moment –
small bag hung on the wall of her room, red clock, cup
light, ticket, unroll of flag behind her head – alerts

us to this, this, and see …this! how can we not notice
asleep as we are, how it is our attention the world
craves. see, Valentine – red note of her name – lift Rita

the dog a weight in her arms, soft whimper, caress, blood
sticky on the road, on her fingers. see how love saves us

Ivo's House

Prague 1993

we sleep for a month on the broken sofa
in the curtained room heavy with dust

the abandoned wedding furniture old oak
carved with wheat sheaves and harvest

mammals – mouse and hare, weasel
fox – all touch, a containment of touch

dark with the shadow's, the daytime's hands
the gowns of night. did I say abandoned? I mean

an attempt at forgetting, a turning away
like the mausoleum on the hill we climb to

impossible path lost under bracken and fern
until the sky clears on a temple of stone

I will put you in this room, love, layered
under light creeping through curtains

burnt by the sun, harrowed by the moon
threads wormed to filaments, particles

become air, become breath. on the wedding
chest the mouse creeps its sheaf of wheat

the fox arches its back, the hare sits up
the weasel ripples in the river of dark

they turn their eyes upon us as naked
on the couch we weave our animal selves

Intervention (iii)

Mirror

after Andrei Tarkovsky, 'Mirror' (1975)

walls fall in water
the room collapses
a man calls at the gate
how beautiful you are
my sister, my lover

yellow heads of corn
gold backs of finches
feeding on thistles
fire in the memory
burning through

to where self folds
to self and the child
holds in potential
the adult like a yolk
within the white

what is it to watch
your past unspool
as if time could be
gathered like wheat
at the close of summer

stacked in sheaves
in barns where in corners
shadows collect?
one part of us moves
forward into history

one part moves us
back into the still rooms
where we walk
like artists constructing
fragments into dreams

Sarajevo/Leeds

1996

we couldn't be with you
in Sarajevo
but watched instead the film
of the women
raped in the war

women like you and I
one day making coffee
preparing for work, the next
dragged from their homes
by neighbours. this dissolution

could happen to any of us
to you there, in your sunlit
room watching dust spiral
as morning gathers
below your window

traffic stutters on the road
and the twenty-first century
moves into view
harbouring a halt, a glitch
like a horse hamstrung

the moon arrested
red horse of time
white horse of history
we sit in these rooms
occupying moments

that fan into lifetimes
each quarter lived in utero
like the women I see
always in my mind
like so much

that can never be
unseen – headscarves
faded with sun, faces
cadenced with tears
all our mirrors

II

Intervention (iv)

Cleaning the Bones
after Marina Abramović, 'Balkan Baroque' (1997)

in a dark hall the artist in a white dress
sits amidst a hill of bones. white dress

white bones, bloodied. *you cannot wash
the blood from your hands, cannot wash*

> *the shame of war from the bones*

> it is summer in Venice and hot, hot

the heat brings worms from the bones
as you enter the hall the smell of bones

greets you like a sonic wave from a shell
dropped amidst the living. they are shells

> spirits of the dead floating like hands

> of white smoke above the city

these bones transmuting under the hands
of the artist, bone shadow to bloodied hands

to glistening pile all grades of white, a prism
stripped of light. the artist dances, a prism

> shifting in and out of dark, of light

> cat's black eye-slit, flickering eye

daughter hung between mother, father, light
of their eyes, their hand's offering of light

what can an artist give but their work
bloodied with bones, their hand's work?

        the city in summer is hot, hot. in the eye-

        slit of a dark hall an artist cleans the bones

the bone worms, the stink, the blood
on her hands, until all is light. the blood

is lifted from us and what remains
                            is bones

January

since you left it has rained, rained
and the earth is soft as chocolate
I stand under the oak tree planted
at your birth, look up through branches'

close-grained wetness, rain-dripped
from dark tips. your year starts
with fire, koalas in rescuer's arms
hands held out like black stars

after you were born you spoke
a dolphin language, whistles and clicks
broadcast through the night like sonar
now you map sea currents as they warm

swim the dead white forests. when you
call the ocean is in your voice, its despair
I listen, around me the tree slumbers
slow-hearted, as rain ticks in my hair

February

a bright day, fug of too-early
midges. I put my hand to the trunk
and tune-in, as if the tree is a radio
and I can hear you, down under

but there is only this stirring
of warmth and beneath it, a guttural
language, rainwater in the channels
of the road, a transfusion. that time

I nearly lost you in the womb, blood
bright as poster paint on the insides
of my thighs. woozy all month
as you held on in your element

and the cervix healed its wound
the tree speaks through my palms
still, still, it says, tingling the skin
as deep in the roots the sap rises

March

this early in the season the tree holds
its leaves tight, crumpled in the wind
like tissue paper. I listen for its heart
sleeping in the shadow of the wall

where in spring a collapsed deer fold
is pressed with bluebells. where you are
summer is on the wane, and winter
will soon frost the eucalyptus

when will I see you? I ask, and the tree
replies *wait, wait; this is the waiting time*
sickness blows across continents
and the world closes like a bud

a wind picks up from behind the hill
a song through dry leaves. I hold
the tip-quiver of a branch and the tree
shakes down inside me

Intervention (v)

Flag

after Marina Abramović, 'Rhythm 5' (1974)

I set burning
a ring of twelve stars
laid in the grass like hands
at the centre

my avatar in old clothes
this is art
who will see it
in these days

of singularity?
a drone sparks alarm
in a distant tower
and a flower

opens in a blue
interior where lit faces
flicker and stare
dream-zone

of our commensurate
age. from the bedroom
window I film
through my phone

petroleum fumes
communicate a hiss
like the letting of gas
from a stove

at the core fake
head, arms, legs
the puffed-out torso
bubble and singe

I am at once alive
and dead, down
there in the grass
and leaning too far

over the windowsill
heat on my face
the ends of my
hair curling

the stars turn
to black threads
then streamers
a calligraphy

like bird flight
and the white
morning burns
to a black noon

as constellations
look down
dispassionate
from their houses

April

small brown buds, some in clusters
cloven, faun's hooves. tree a slow
dance in a separate dimension
reach and open, says the tree's aura

the sun is here. in the woods, someone
is shooting. a deer family appear
in the fields' long grass. remember
when you were small and we saw

the faun sleeping in its basket of reeds?
the deer pause, ears tuned as forks
if only I could sketch them, but they are
off in one bound, an exclamation

tree reaches skyward like a child
waving at a plane. I press my heart
outwards to meet the tree's albumen
and time folds us into its field

May

slow awakening, buds furred
like the foot of a weasel at harvest time
its tail dried and packed into a bale
springing into my hand, an amulet

and today, gold and burnt sienna clusters
broken out all over, downy and crimped
as new-hatched chicks. bluebells
flock the roots, the perfume of their throats

damp arias, and you in those cotton
dungarees you wore all summer, bending
your head to tear fistfuls of flowers
and cast them to the air, your hands stars

when you call, your three am face grainy
on the laptop screen, I take you to the garden
where the tree waves its gold crown
at not one plane crossing the cerulean

June

full bodied now, tree has grown
sun rests, happiness on its canopy
after the thunderstorm, leaves
voice notes into sung dimensions

I draw an outline from several angles
this way, the tree leans towards me
blushing greenly. from the wall
it is skywards, aloof, an arabesque

how far away you are, how close
we facetime, your eyes hooped
with tiredness, hair a mess. still
on the kitchen doorpost, the pencil

marks your growth. if felled tree
could show each year's correspondence
as if hearing, the tree reaches out –
a gasp in the throat, a loop of hope

Intervention (vi)

Presence

after Marina Abramović, 'The Artist is Present' (2012)
for J

what happens when we sit
is that presence appears
in the unspoken closeness
chemical dabs on the air
undetected in the space

perceives the other body
with tears that well and fall
opens like a slab of rock
in the long ago, in the deep
millennia since we dwelled

flickering against the wall
where only the face of the
of our colony, the familiar
where your gaze is a fire
the heart, every tissue, every

to dissolve like thoughts
you look and look as your
the body enters a process of
no longer empty but now
on the mouth, lips parted

where presence is we are
made more than ourselves
existence we might name
of colour that becomes white
the translucence of the shell

together with the silence
like desire between lovers
of bodies in proximity
droplets of scent almost
between chairs as body

eyes globules of rain swollen
as in the chest the heart
shifted from a cave door
of our unconscious where
in dark nights with fire

across our faces, throats, hands
other was perceived, faces
strange in the caress of flame
of connectives that trigger
bone, down to the marrow

on particles of breath
eyes fracture like facets and
osmosis across the gap that is
a communion, a trace of salt
tongue dense with saliva

remade in the other, we are
where a third entity enters
love or angel or the prism
albumen and yolk within
that contains us all whole

July

all month the tree is decked with wasps
I stand a moment within the canopy
as their lit bodies busy. tree is a mother
calling them to her ecstasy. all her nubs

nobbles and grazes, calyxes. stretch marks
where a palm branches to five hands
the almost-lichen of skin. and here too
the boy-spirit, russet hermaphrodite

when you were small, I would lift you
into the leaves to see the spangle galls'
tiny haberdashery, miniature disco balls
yellow nets for baby wasps. long strands

of your blond hair caught the sunlight
between branches, the weight of you
against me, heels pressing my thighs
as the hot day pressures my heart, my blood

August

summer's rush of leaves stipple
with wasp eggs, oak apples, and droop
yellowed in patches or spotted
the one acorn is an aborted nub

small face in a hood. after your birth
the blue wool cap the midwife gave me
to warm your head. I dream of you
as a child, your presence weighted

with your absence. I am a thought
in time, your birth-day nested inside
like an egg. *come*, tree says, *into
my world*, where time still moves

in this roundel, slowly. above us
spiderwebs tip-toe between branches
refract light like a window, one thrown
thread anchoring us to the Earth

September

rain comes, a drip-drip symphony
tree is all itself without me. I draw
raindrop trails on glass, my portrait
in a globe. art is activity in seeing

an interior energy. beneath bark
tree's heart is a slow diminution
of time, each breath an exchange
of moisture and carbon

when we are gone, Earth will enter
this steady tick, this geological drift
Earth is ever-dreaming without us
suspended in green abstraction

you are here at last, and the hours
fold like origami as daylight unveils
leaves, branches, trunk become fauns
maidens, a ring of dancers

Intervention (vii)

Arrow

after Marina Abramović, 'Rest Energy' (1980)

I am poised in trust, trembling
       the arrow in your bow
       arrow tip in my fingertips
held to my chest

where the metronome
       scatters rapid beats
       little breathless bird   caught   in its moments
before death

you flicker in and out of light
       the blackout/whiteout of knowing/not knowing

       and I stand helpless

lean into what energy remains
if I place my concentration in stillness
       but always the heart moves towards its rest

you are there/not there
       and if I reach out my other hand
to bring you near
            the balance between us will collapse

October

begins in rain, grass sodden
leaves brown and spotted
yellow dropsied, clouds a veil
but now the beauty of the morning

stuns the sky and it falls apart
pieces of blue. tree hoards
bees, flies, a bluebottle sunning
its wings, abdomen an opal

why do I feel like crying? scent
of laundry a mile away or this
eucalyptus, out of its continent
sniffing, I walk the garden boundary

and after you leave, the violence
of the loss of you again. tree scented
with the incense of its being becomes
the centre, this censor teeming

November

all month leaves turn burnt sugar
caramel, rust. tree's voice is stilled
grounding the heart's beats slow
between the root's dark clasps

for two weeks tree is a confused
body holding tightly to its gown
then frost comes and tree drops
soft drifts of hands in the grass

you are far from me again, sailing
the warmed surface of the Earth
your ship a light cast amidst darkness
I climb a stone wedged into the hip

of the wall and listen to the wind flip
press the tenderness of skin above
my breast against bark and let down
my hair, grown all this year to a nest

December

lovely in the cold sun, tree whispers
vestments of old leaves, air between
branches, spaces of intimacy. the year
ends and tree settles its debts

to the sun, to the wind, to the rain
we bow down to the soil turning
with worms. my hands to this bark
skin-like and cool, scored, papery

my mouth to this gulp of absence
my body to this body. I hear
the tick of blood, lay an ear
to the silence as tree signs off

with a sigh. across the sky
contrail of geese, white on white
like messages in secret ink I send
you folded into gifts. like gifts

Intervention (viii)

Seven Gates

after Marina Abramović, 'Gates and Portals' (2023)

enter here then, bind your eyes and take my hand
let me show you what thought does, freed from
                                              the body

through the skin of our palms the exchange of sweat
traverse of energy into wrist, forearm, in the belly
                                              a turning

flight into the chest. the gallery opens into whiteness
with entry points that are also exits, doorways. at the
                                              first gate

divest your jewels, what you hold against loss false
emblems. lose all noise but the wingbeats inside you
                                              on your ears

two soft black cups, lost birds. at the second gate
your crown loosens and drops. reach inwards to your feet
                                              bright stones

they will bring you back. the third gate is an opening
in the dark. hear the breath of our companions
                                              who have gone

before, feather on feather like hands greeting air
at the fourth gate notice how the place where your
                                              ribs part

thrums and lifts, like a lover cupping you in the first
hours of the morning, as a musician draws in ecstasy
                                              her bow

across strings so taut you ache for release. at the fifth
gate lose all vestments and float, a blown egg held
                                        in the hand

where you see into the shell of yourself. the sixth gate
requires nakedness. peel like a gold seed shucked
                                        glistening

at the seventh gate time's water spins to stillness
stirred eye of the hurricane. all is blue chinks in glass
                                              glints

off pools. in the dry bottom of a well the future waits
with the past, a child looking towards stars. you are
                                        nothing now

but a word of love spoken before dawn, a cloud-lit sun
luminous as a visitation, a gasp of brightness falling
                                        to be reborn

III

missives from 2050

1.

tonight   the storm
    plays her concerto
on the strings of the hill

        the clouds are indigo   midnight
    against slate
        wet with rain

the roof rattles   the window frame
    admits the wind

        the dissolution of wind

2.

the day is cyan   de-oxygenated blue
                  to the horizon
      where trees

    hold their conference

      do you
    remember the birds –
      do they still
    gather   ghosts?

3.

I write this   thirty years away

                                              my love

    Earth

                    now

every particle   we save
    from the blue   o   cerulean azure teal

              the tyranny of blue

4.

everywhere   the voice of the air
    my hands old
             but in my ear
the world's
        remembered music

thrown on the wind, a crow speaks
    with a human voice

        across the field
        the flicker of starlings –

        on/off, on/off as they lift, alight, lift

5.

remember   when
    we hired a boat
                                         rowed
  too far out
                        to be recalled
the waters   swallowing our
         voices
         birds

    with no Earth
    to land upon

6.

    I walk out into the field
  once my garden   where the walls
have fallen
    to   where the spring
      pulses and births

  slip my hand into its open

7.

a figure walks   shade of
    a woman   I leave
                    little bells

      stones
seven gold disks

   of my dream

8.

how will we know
     what will be reborn?   lay a prayer

where the waters   become a
       mirror

                  step into

9.

the other world   membrane

  viscous as birth

    your face

  as if we have just   spoken

    the screen   turning blue
      with the sky

        behind you

10.

debris of centuries   pile up
    what we leave

  behind us

    love

   and memory
I would like to tell you of a pristine

   Earth cleansed of us   but

11.

daily I tread the meniscus   of water
    feet bare
        in the inches deep   an offering
                                        some days

    the mud   embalms my toes   my ankles

        blue veined   nuptial
                                  oh

12.

one day   I will join you

        goddess   child

    lover   friend
            the spring that joined
                the house of my heart

                              to yours

but for now   Earth spins

                            holding me

13.

what is Earth　　　　　　but an ossuary
　　　of the lost?　　we collect　　　　like stones

　　　　　in a tributary　　　　silted
　　with neglect　　　hold the shining ones
　　　　　　　in our palms

14.

what did I say
　　　　　　　of the music of the birds?　　　　gone

　　only the wind　　　　　　　　　across the water

　　　　　what sound is that?　　a susurration

　　　　　of loneliness

15.

I could sing   but my voice
                                            melts on air
        I open my mouth   hear
     only the Earth's   notation
        a five-finger exercise
                    the wind's sonata

  on my skin

16.

today   at dawn   the crows return
    only   echoes
                           sun spots
              shadows
        hands opening   wings

17.

do you remember   the magpies

                                         that wet year

         the garden hostage   to their
  squabbles
         the white-winged   crow
         a sign

                                              ah now
  the ghost magpie   where did he go?

18.

I must speak   now   of the trees

        how their leaves   unfurled

    each spring   arching towards   sun/
        light   air   oh

the unfold   of their   want

19.

                        I am become   water/

            land

     lie down   in the surrender

         of this

                  gift   goddess

she comes now   and

                        what song

               sifts

20.

listen   there is another

                                frequency

     always
     below   the air

                          beneath

        the water

              within   the rock

where   the spring   finds

  voice

  the world's   unspoken

                            desire

Notes

This work was inspired by Krzysztof Kieślowski's seminal trilogy of film masterpieces, *Three Colours: Red, White and Blue* (1992, 1994, 1994) which explore the essential nature of human connection across the three themes of liberty, equality and fraternity. Kieślowski set out to celebrate the European Union, but in filming his final work, he realised that the only thing that matters is how we connect.

The Ishtar Gate was built by King Nebuchadnezzar in Babylon, modern day Iraq, around 599 BC and honours the goddess Ishtar. A reconstruction stands in the Pergamon Museum, Berlin, after excavations in the early part of the twentieth century uncovered fragments of the gate and processional way. German archaeologists took many treasures back to Berlin, including most of the friezes which lined the processional way. France and Britain also stole parts of the original Ishtar Gate and took them to the Louvre and the British Museum. In 2002, Iraq appealed to Berlin for the gate to be returned but this appeal was refused.

In the most famous myth of Ishtar/Innana, she is called by her sister Ereshkigal to the underworld where she must pass through seven gates, losing all her worldly acquisitions as she goes. In the underworld, Ishtar is struck dead and brought back to life after three days when she is permitted to return to the upper world. But she must leave her husband, Dumuzid, behind as her replacement. Eventually he is allowed to return to the world for part of the year.

My poem at the beginning of this book attempts to re-situate the Ishtar Gate in mythical time, where it stands 'firm as a mountain' as Nebuchadnezzar's inscription on the gate reads.

In my version, the Ishtar Gate remains intact and in situ as a universal symbol of the way to rebirth and renewal.

In 'Leningrad' the Russian poet Anna Akhmatova awaits the arrival of the first part of her triptych 'Poem without a Hero'. On one such night, she kept an egg for her friend, the poet Osip Mandelstam, who died after incarceration in one of Stalin's Gulags.

'Berlin' quotes from Helene Cixious (Helene Cixious, *Stigmata*, Routledge, 1998), Ingeborg Bachmann ('Message', *Songs in Flight: The Collected Poems of Ingeborg Bachmann*, Marsilio, 1994) and Wim Wenders (*Wings of Desire*, 1986).

The interventions in book II are inspired by and respond to the work of Serbian performance artist Marina Abramović. It was my engagement with Abramović's work that opened a new way of thinking about the collection and allowed the central theme of human love, desire and connection to find its voice.

'Cleaning the Bones' quotes Marina Abramović in an interview discussing Balkan Baroque.

Acknowledgements

Acknowledgments are due to the editors of the following journals where some of these poems, or versions of these poems, first appeared: *Bad Lilies* (online), *London Magazine*, *The Manchester Review* (online), *Poetry Ireland Review*, *Swerve* (Ireland).

Thank you to The Society of Authors for an Author's Foundation Grant in 2019 which facilitated a visit to Berlin and the writing of the early part of this book.

Thank you to Mona Arshi, who read early drafts of 'Berlin' and encouraged me to continue. Thank you to Jodie Hollander, who reminded me of the Ishtar Gate, and gave me my title. To Ed Reiss for helping me see the clarity of things. Thank you to Catherine Spooner and Veronica Turiano from our Lancaster Writer's Group for commenting on early drafts. Thanks as ever to the team at Pavilion Poetry, and to my editor Deryn Rees-Jones, who always sees the way, and makes it possible.

Love and thank you to all those – lovers, artists, colleagues, poets, family, friends – who have supported and inspired me during the writing of this book. You know who you are.